HE SAVES

CU00924025

HE SAVES

THE ASSURANCE
OF SALVATION
THROUGH FAITH

 R.T. KENDALL

Authentic

Authentic Publishing
We welcome your questions and comments

USA   PO Box 444, 285 Lynnwood Ave, Tyrone, GA, 30290
       authentic@stl.org or www.authenticbooks.com
UK   9 Holdom Avenue, Bletchley, Milton Keynes, Bucks, MK1 1QR, UK
       www.authenticmedia.co.uk
India Logos Bhavan, Medchal Road, Jeedimetla Village, Secunderabad
       500 055, A.P.

He Saves
ISBN-10: 1-85078-361-6
ISBN-13: 978-1-85078-361-9

Copyright © 1988 by R.T. Kendall

First printed in 1988

Published in 2006 by Authentic
All rights reserved. No part of this book may be reproduced in any form without
permission in writing from the publisher, except in the case of brief quotations
embodied in critical articles or reviews.

All scripture quotations, unless otherwise indicated, are taken from the HOLY
BIBLE, NEW INTERNATIONAL VERSION®. NIV®. Copyright ©1973, 1978,
1984 by International Bible Society. Used by permission of Zondervan. All
rights reserved.

Scriptures marked KJV are taken from the Holy Bible, King James Version.

Cover design: Paul Lewis
Editorial team: KJ Larson and Megan Kassebaum

Printed and bound in India by
OM Books, P.O. Box 2014, Secunderabad 500 003
E-mail: printing@ombooks.org

Other books by R.T. Kendall

Once Saved, Always Saved

All's Well that Ends Well

Justification by Works

The Way of Wisdom

Jonah

God of the Bible

Does Jesus Care

God Meant It for Good

Calvin and English Calvinism

CONTENTS

INTRODUCTION

The following illustration should demonstrate the importance of getting it right on the biblical teaching of salvation. A jet plane takes off from John F. Kennedy Airport in New York heading for London. The pilot is only barely off course but continues eastward in the general direction. The slight deviation seems harmless at first, but six hours later, instead of circling over London's Heathrow Airport, his plane is flying over Spain!

This sort of thing can happen (alas, I fear, has happened) concerning the biblical doctrine of salvation. We may start in the right direction, but the slightest alteration from God's revealed plan will, sooner or later, take us a long way from his intended destination.

Three verses, Romans 1:16–18, form the foundation for this little book. I have chosen these verses for two reasons: first, because Paul's Epistle to the Romans is the purest and profoundest statement to be found on the gospel; second, these verses provide a clear and carefully worded outline of that Epistle. If we can grasp Romans 1:16–18 we will be well on our way to understanding the rest of Romans—and we can avoid getting off course in our understanding of salvation. The whole of Romans is to be seen as an unfolding of Romans 1:16–18.

Why should Romans be so important? Is not the gospel found in the Corinthian letters, Galatians, and others? Of course it is. But in most of his letters Paul addresses those who have already been exposed to his teaching. There was no need to "spoon feed" them again. In any case, he was dealing with special needs and problems in the churches in his other letters and therefore simply enlarged upon points they had already been taught.

But Paul had never been to Rome. He envisaged going there and decided to write these Christians a letter before he arrived and state exactly what he believed. It would also seem that no other apostle had yet been to Rome. He therefore took nothing for granted and wanted them to know apostolic truth. This explains the detail he goes into which is not as clearly found in the other letters Paul wrote. It therefore also shows what the other churches had been taught by him prior to his writing to them.

Why not begin with one of the four Gospels, or at least the Gospel of John? In a small book like this too much space would be needed merely to differentiate those teachings of Jesus that refer to salvation from those that demonstrate how the Christian life is to be lived. What is more, if we accept Paul's claim that his own teaching was but revealed to him by Jesus Himself (Galatians 1:12), we are therefore getting a distillation, if not clarification, of the four Gospels when we read Paul. For Jesus would only give to Paul what would elucidate, say, the Parables, never contradict them.

The doctrine of salvation is the most important teaching there is, for a correct understanding of the person of Jesus is an essential part of salvation. Jesus came that the world might be "saved" (John 3:17). This teaching becomes very personal for each of us, for we must all come to terms with where we shall spend eternity.

CHAPTER ONE

WHAT IS THE GOSPEL?

"For I am not ashamed of the gospel of Christ: for it is the power of God unto salvation, to every one that believeth; to the Jew first, and also to the Greek." (Romans 1:16 KJV)

If you are not a Christian, I will show you how to become one. And if you are a Christian, perhaps this will be an important clarification concerning the true nature of the gospel. Romans 1:16 is one of the great verses not just of Romans but in the whole Bible, and every new Christian who sets his heart on memorizing the Scriptures should put this near the top of the list.

In this verse the apostle Paul says four things:

1. What it is he is not ashamed of—the gospel. The word gospel means "good news."

2. What that gospel is—It is the power of God with particular reference to "salvation."

3. The condition that releases that power—faith. "To everyone that believes."

4. The scope of the gospel—that is, to whom it is offered—"To the Jew first, and also to the Greek." In other words, to everybody.

Two things are urgently needed today: that there should be a people who are unashamed of the gospel and that great care be taken in clarifying to people what that gospel is. The devil hates the gospel, and he will do anything to divert us from it, even ever so slightly, and the way he does it sometimes seems so innocent.

The devil knows just how to bring in things, even good things, that camouflage the gospel. One of the greatest enemies of the gospel is the subtle but superficially plausible attempt to *destigmatize* the gospel. The gospel inherently contains a stigma. There's nothing more offensive than the blood which Jesus shed when He died on the cross. There is no greater offense than the premise that a person is actually saved from the wrath of God by simple trust in the blood of Jesus, and the devil will do anything to get us away from that. The offence shows itself by our being ashamed, embarrassed and afraid: afraid that in putting *all* of our eggs into one basket, namely the gospel, we will be left "high and dry;" that mere faith in the gospel is not enough.

Perhaps the best way we know what we really believe is by asking: what do we trust when the time comes to die? It is possible to be saved five minutes before we die, but only a fool would wait till then. For first of all we don't know that our mind will be clear then, and we don't know whether our heart will not be hardened by then, and in any case we may not get a five minute warning!

However, if you knew that you were going to die in five minutes, is it possible to be saved? Yes. But how? Well, obviously it's too late then to do anything more than to lean on the mere mercy of God. *What is true five minutes before you die is true now,* even if you have thirty years left to live. Paul believed this, and thus said, "I am not ashamed of the gospel."

The effort to destigmatize the gospel is either to dilute it or add to it so that people generally are not offended or embarrassed by it any more. In Paul's day there were those who substituted obedience to the Law of Moses for simple faith in Jesus Christ. Known as Judaisers, they even insisted that Gentile Christians be circumcised. They said, "Don't think for one minute you are going to get to heaven just by trusting what Jesus did on the cross. Do you really think you can be safe with that? There must be a condition, and that is, that you promise to obey the Law; *then* you can know that you are going to go to heaven."

Then there were those who began to think that faith alone in the gospel *was* too easy, and feared that immoral living would be the consequence. Paul of course had to deal with that, and he did so in Romans 6. He had done so when he wrote the letter to the church at Galatia (cf.

Galatians 5:13ff). Ten years later, having dealt with the problem at Galatia, having also seen problems in the church at Corinth and the church at Thessalonica, he is now writing to a people that he has never seen, saying, "I am not ashamed of the gospel." There were those who were ashamed, for to them it was a stigma, even a danger, to believe that you are saved by what Jesus did on the cross. But not for Paul.

We still see the "gospel-plus" in many quarters. On one extreme there are those who deny the infallibility of Scripture, which is always the result of attempting to destigmatize the gospel. At the other extreme there are still those who say, "Yes, we believe in justification by faith, but it is given upon the condition of obedience to the Law." There you are, right back to the very thing Paul had to correct in the early church. It always cuts the very jugular vein of the gospel.

One difficulty with the view that you are saved upon condition of good behavior is that you will never have assurance that you are saved. Who among us will ever feel holy enough to be able to say, "Yes, I now believe I'm saved"? That is inviting self-righteousness in its most blatant form.

In between these two extremes there is the "social" gospel which places the emphasis on caring for people but at the expense of the simple gospel. The crucial issues today, we are told, are abortion, or poverty, or nuclear war, or the need to get involved in politics to make sure a certain person is elected.

There's another subtle attempt: the "signs and wonders" gospel. I'm not against it. But it is embraced by those, I fear, who aren't always content with Paul's heartbeat. Some feel that in order to authenticate the Bible, people need to see something "happen." They think that this emphasis on signs and wonders is the best way to stimulate Christians and convince the world. Sometimes it is referred to, I think unfairly, as the "gospel of the kingdom." But here's Paul who says, "I am not ashamed of the gospel." The simple gospel.

Then there are those who emphasize prosperity. This is the way to reach a lot of people because most of us want to get ahead and pay our bills and improve our standard of living. "God wants you rich," say these people.

The gospel is primarily the revelation of God's power. "It is the power of God." As Harry Kilbride says, it takes more power to save a soul than to create the universe, because to save a soul the Creator of the universe had to become weak and die on a cross. This is why the apostle Paul could say, "The preaching of the cross is to them that perish foolishness; but unto us which are saved it is the *power of God"* (1 Corinthians 1:18). To those who are called, whether a Jew or Greek, Christ is "the power of God" (1 Corinthians 1:24*).* According to Paul the very person of Jesus is the power of God. He therefore also says, "I am not ashamed of the gospel of Christ: for *it* is the power of God." The gospel is Christ!

Paul clarifies what he means by God's power: it is the power of God with reference to *salvation.* Some may wish Paul had said something else, such as, "The gospel is the power of God with reference to creation." The subtle attempt to camouflage the gospel here is sometimes known as the "cultural mandate." It is an idea that the second chapter of Genesis is a mandate to restore the order of unfallen creation; whether it be through ecology, emphasizing anti-abortion, or the evil of euthanasia. But, however valid, it is still a diversion from the gospel. Paul did not say, "I am not ashamed of the gospel of Christ for it is the power of God with reference to creation."

Some might wish that Paul had said the gospel is the power of God with reference to prophecy. There's always a lot of interest if you can talk about "last things," predictions of the future, what is happening in Israel today or what will happen to the Jews. There are those who like the idea of a "prophetic word." They are fascinated by ministers who will say to their congregations, "I have a word of knowledge that someone here has an abscessed tooth." Or, "Someone has got a pain in their side," or "Someone here is fearful that tomorrow you might not have a job when you get into work." This sort of thing can be almost like astrology; people are interested in what will speak to them directly, and there are always a lot of people *unashamed* of things like that. Paul said, "I am not ashamed of the gospel, for it is the power of God with reference to salvation."

We may have wished that Paul had said it is the power of God with reference to healing. No one likes to see healing take place more than I do. We have a prayer meeting at our church every Sunday evening, and we have the anointing of oil, we pray for the sick, and I love to see people healed. But that's not the gospel. To some it is. Paul didn't think so. He didn't say, "The gospel is the power of God with reference to healing."

Some might wish he had said, "the power of God with reference to demons." There are those who emphasize casting out devils, and want all problems to be solved by uncovering what demon you have got. But, that's not the gospel. Paul says, "I am not ashamed of the gospel, for it is the power of God with reference to *salvation.*"

We are living in an age, then, when there are all kinds of attempts to introduce elements that will interest people, and destigmatize the gospel. To talk about being "saved" is so old-fashioned, but it is the only thing that will matter when it is time to die. God could heal you, and you could lose your soul. God could deliver you and even make you rich. But you could still face an eternity without God, without hope; and eternity lasts a long time.

This generation knows almost nothing about the wrath of God. Why did Jesus die on the cross? Was there no other way we could be saved? Why wasn't it by the Sermon on the Mount which He taught? Or the ethic of loving your enemy, and doing good to those who mistreat you? Why did He have to die? It is because of sin, and God had to deal with sin.

Do we take lightly our ability to lie about people, hurt people, walk over people to get ahead, pulling strings, and doing things that we know are hurting other lives? What about the way we abuse our bodies with drugs, alcohol, or sex? Any sex outside of marriage is an abuse of your body. You may say, "It feels right at the time; it's OK; God understands me." The devil has come in and blinded you to what God thinks. But God hates these things so much that the only way He could forgive them is by sending His Son into the world to die on a cross. The next time you are ready to do something that you know is wrong, remember what it cost God to save men.

When a person is saved it is as though it were a silent thing. That is to say it happens in the heart. But the Bible says there is rejoicing in heaven. Jesus said there is joy in heaven "over one sinner that repenteth, more than over ninety and nine just persons, which need no repentance" (Luke 15:7 KJV). The crucial thing about the gospel is that the power of God unto salvation is released only when you believe, "to everyone that believeth." We might wish that Paul had said it is the power of God to "everyone," period. If he had said that, then everybody would be saved. I would not need to write this book, and we would not need to witness. No, it pleased God through the foolishness of preaching (1 Corinthians 1:21 KJV) to save them that believe, and we must hear the word. What needs to be made absolutely clear is that, though Jesus Christ died on the cross for the Jew and for the Greek, it is effectual *only* for those who *believe.*

Never think that because the gospel is offered to someone he or she automatically has it. Jesus died for all, but not everyone is saved. This power is released on the condition of faith.

There are some who might say, "Paul must have meant it is the power of God to everyone that does good works." To that Paul replies, "To him that worketh is the reward not reckoned of grace, but of debt. But to him that *worketh not,* but believeth on him that justifieth the ungodly, his *faith* is counted for righteousness" (Romans 4:4–5 KJV).

Belief in this gospel can only take place by the Holy Spirit. This makes us vulnerable. Our works—no matter how many, how righteous, or how well intentioned they may be—never, never, never atone for sin. The only thing that atones for sin is the blood that Jesus shed on the cross, and the apostle Paul fought all his life for this. It means putting all of our eggs into one basket.

If you are not a Christian, I must ask you to renounce all hope in your good works. You may be a moral person, and I would not want you to be any other kind of person. But if you are trusting that morality for your salvation, you are just as lost as the most immoral person walking the streets of London or New York. You have got to give up any hope that your morality will save you, and come instead to the place where you see you have got no bargaining power. That is, with God.

I would not even ask you to promise anything. Do you know the hymn "Just as I am Without One Plea"? It was written because at the time there was an ascendancy of the belief that we are saved not by faith alone, but faith *plus* our willingness to do good works. Here came one bold enough to write:

> Just as I am, without one plea
> But that Thy blood was shed for me,
>
> And that Thou bidd'st me come to Thee,
> O Lamb of God, I come.

CHAPTER TWO

THE RIGHTEOUSNESS OF GOD

"For therein is the righteousness of God revealed from faith to faith." (Romans 1:17 KJV)

In the last chapter we saw that the gospel of Christ is the power of God with reference to salvation. We also saw that the releasing of God's power is given to those who believe. Paul elaborates that very point in verse 17, for the next thing he says is this: "therein is the righteousness of God revealed" (KJV).

I want to make clear in this chapter what lies behind this great power that is released when you believe the gospel. It is God's righteousness.

Now Paul might have said, "For therein is the love of God revealed," or "For therein is the mercy of God revealed," or "For therein is the wrath of God revealed." All these things are also revealed in the gospel. But the word he used is "righteousness"—"the righteousness of God."

In the original language (Greek) the word translated "righteousness" actually has two meanings: righteousness, but also "justice." The righteousness or justice of God may seem to be an archaic concept. You may say, "What does that mean to me?" Well, righteousness is what makes God happy. It makes God pleased with the very people He has created but who have turned against Him—that is all of us.

The most important question that we can ever try to answer—and maybe you have never thought to ask this question before—is this: "How can I, a guilty sinner, satisfy the righteousness or justice of God?" After all, the next verse talks about the wrath of God being revealed from heaven against "all ungodliness and unrighteousness of men" (Romans 1:18 KJV).

For all of us by nature are under God's wrath (Ephesians 2:3). Now we may say, "I don't feel anything. If He is angry with me, I can't tell it." I can explain why. The apostle Paul who wrote these words also said that the devil, the "god of this world has blinded" the minds of those who believe not (2 Corinthians 4:4 KJV). We can sin, and it does not bother us. The Holy Spirit alone makes us see that we are abiding under God's wrath.

Once one dies there will not be any difficulty seeing what God thinks of sin. All see it then. But through the preaching of the gospel—when the Spirit applies it, we are given to see this *before* we die. That's why we are saved. Do you think that those who are saved are better than others? Do they look more intelligent? Are they more sophisticated? Why is it that anybody believes this? Why is it that they would die for it? It is because the Holy Spirit has caused them to see what God thinks of sin.

Perhaps you have heard of Martin Luther, a sixteenth-century Roman Catholic monk. God used Romans 1:17 to save his soul. It turned the world upside down for Martin Luther, and the result was that much of the world was changed by the great Reformation.

Luther was able to see that by *justice* the apostle Paul was referring to the "passive" justice of God. "Active" justice would be what one does in order to get satisfaction. Perhaps somebody has done something to you and you want to get even, so you do something to feel better. We once got letters from a man who wanted to know "what you are going to do" about some person. This letter-writer thought that someone had not been treated with enough justice. It is easy for anybody to become preoccupied with wanting to get even with somebody. That is seeking "active" justice.

Passive justice would be getting satisfaction by doing nothing. If that letter-writer, assuming he had a valid case, had let God handle things, he would have got his justice without trying. He therefore would have passively gotten the justice he so earnestly wanted; and he would be totally satisfied.

The Bible basically says two things about God: that He is merciful and that He is just. By merciful it means that God does not want to punish us. By being just He must punish us—because we have all sinned. "All have sinned, and come short of the glory of God" (Romans 3:23 KJV).

Can God be just and merciful at the same time? The answer is yes: He sent His Son into the world and punished Him—the God-man who never sinned—for *our* sins. The prophet Isaiah wrote, "The Lord hath laid on him (Jesus) the iniquity of us all" (Isaiah 53:6 KJV). He who knew no sin was "made sin" (2 Corinthians 5:21 KJV), thus satisfying God's justice so that He could be merciful to us. This is the heart of the gospel: God punished Jesus for what we did.

But that was God's active justice at work. God shows His anger by pouring out His wrath upon Jesus. This happened when Jesus cried on the cross, "My God, my God, why have you forsaken me?" (Matthew 27:46).

What is God's "passive" justice—which Luther perceived to be the meaning of God's righteousness (justice) in Romans 1:17? It is when God did nothing, as it were; merely getting satisfaction by our own very *faith*. God's active justice was executing His wrath toward Jesus; His passive justice was seeing our faith.

Passive justice, then, is what we do to satisfy God. How extraordinary to think that God, whose wrath is hovering over us, can be satisfied by something we do! Paul combines these two concepts—active justice and passive justice—by a carefully designed phrase: "Faith to faith." "The righteousness of God (is) revealed from faith to faith." Those words in and by themselves are not very clear at first, and we do not know what Paul means for sure until we see the next time he uses that phrase in Chapter 3 verses 21 and 22, when he says that the righteousness of God is revealed by the "faith of Jesus Christ unto all and upon all them that believe" (KJV). So the first time he used the expression "righteousness of God" he just said it was revealed "from faith to faith." Romans 3:22 tells us exactly what he means by "faith to faith."

Paul thus talks about two subjects of faith, the faith of Jesus and our faith. Paul's expression "faith of Jesus Christ" typifies all that Jesus did *for* us by His sinless life: never sinning, fulfilling the law, believing perfectly. Jesus never doubted God. Jesus did everything God wanted Him to do. Though He was God, He was equally man. As a man, He had faith, and He was our substitute.

Faith always produces obedience. Jesus's faith was a perfect faith, so it produced a perfect obedience. We are therefore said to be saved by Christ's obedience (Romans 5:19). For Jesus had to fulfill the law, as He said He would do in Matthew 5:17.

The law of Moses may be understood in three ways: moral (the Ten Commandments), civil (the way the nation of Israel was to be governed), and ceremonial (the ancient way of worshipping God). When Jesus fulfilled the law He did so by keeping it *all*.

Jesus was our substitute, then, not only by His death on the cross but by His life. This is why Paul said, "For if, when we were enemies, we were reconciled to God by the death of his Son, much more, being reconciled, we shall be saved by his life" (Romans 5:10 KJV). In a word: Jesus believed for us; He obeyed for us. When He was crucified God's wrath was actively executed upon Jesus, our substitute. This then was God's active justice. But it was necessary that Jesus was pure and spotless (without sin), just as the lamb for sacrifice under the law must be without spot or blemish (cf. Exodus 12:5). This is why John the Baptist hailed Jesus as the "Lamb of God" who would take away the sin of the world (John 1:29).

C. H. Spurgeon insisted that there is no gospel "without substitution or satisfaction." These two words should be incorporated into our theological vocabulary. By substitution it means *Jesus took our place.* By satisfaction it means that God's justice was satisfied by what Jesus did.

All this is what Paul meant by the "first" faith (when he said that the righteousness of God is revealed from "faith to faith"). When Paul thus uses the expression "faith to faith" he says, as it were, "this is the clue, this is the key." The clue is clearly unveiled in Chapter 3 when he says that what Jesus did must also be affirmed by us. *We must believe it.*

No wonder Martin Luther was so thrilled when he discovered that our very faith is referring to the passive justice of God. That there is actually something we can do to make God happy: believe the gospel, and believe that Jesus paid our debt.

The "second" faith in this "faith to faith" phrase, then, is *our* faith. Notice carefully how Paul puts it in Romans 3:22: "Even the righteousness of God which is by faith of Jesus Christ unto all and upon *all them that believe*" (KJV). Jesus believed, yes; but we too must believe. We are justified by His faith, yes; but we too must have faith or we will not be justified. Paul made this precise point in Galatians 2:16: "we have believed *in* Jesus Christ, that we might be justified *by* the faith *of* Christ" (KJV).

To put it another way: what Jesus did for us was all that is required in terms of a substitute. God requires of mankind a perfect obedience to the Law of God so that in thought, word, and deed we never break the law. God requires of us a perfect worship of Him; that we worship Him with all our heart, soul, mind, and strength. God requires of us that we love our neighbor as ourselves and that we do this not only in deed but in thought, and in word. You may say, "Well, if God requires that of me, I think I'm in a bit of trouble." Quite, that is why we need a substitute.

Alternatively, when we hear this at first, our natural reaction may be to say, "I think I've done that. Let's see, I'm trying to live a good life. I'm trying to be obedient; I'm trying to do all these things." And what we often do when we hear this is to convince ourselves that somehow we are righteous. The apostle Paul knew that we would have to be taught that we are sinners. This teaching is done

21

through the declaration of God's word and by the power of the Holy Spirit applying what we hear. As we hear it we are made to see that we are in fact sinners.

When Paul said the righteousness of God is revealed from faith to faith there are those who may well wish he had said something else. For example, that the righteousness of God is revealed from faith to *works*. "Oh yes, Jesus died for us on the cross, but now we must do good to show that we believe in Him." Some will even say, "You are justified by faith, but the only way you know you have faith is by works." If anybody accepts that, they are going to trust their works every time. But Paul did not say "from faith to works," he said "from faith to faith."

Some may wish Paul had said, "The righteousness of God is revealed from faith to baptism." But Paul did not say that. Baptism does not save anyone.

There are those who say, "If only Paul had said, 'The righteousness of God is revealed from faith to morality.'" You may want to feel that all that is required of you is clean living. You will feel better for it, because your conscience gives you peace when you stop doing the things that abuse God's Law. But you may take that good feeling as somehow being a green light that all is well with you. That is not what Paul said!

Some may wish that Paul said, "The righteousness of God is revealed from faith to church membership." But you can join the church and be lost.

Some think that the gospel is revealed from faith to social involvement. They think they are really doing well if they can prevent an X-rated film from being shown on television, or challenge economic injustice. I am certainly not against doing this. I thank God for all that is done to bring health to the nation, but there are people who actually think they must be saved because they are doing things like this.

Another person may wish that Paul had said, "The righteousness of God is revealed from faith to being born in a Christian home." Billy Sunday used to say being born in a Christian home will no more make you a Christian than being born in a stable will make you a cow!

Some may wish that Paul had said, "The righteousness of God is revealed from faith to sincerity." "It doesn't matter of which religion you are as long as you are sincere." But sincerity will not save you. Proverbs 14:12 tells us, "There is a way which seemeth right unto a man, But the end thereof are the ways of death" (KJV). Now I do not know of anything scarier than this. You can think, "God knows I'm sincere" and yet be lost. You can lose your soul because trusting your sincerity is a subtle form of trusting your own self-righteousness.

Some may wish Paul had said, "The righteousness of God is revealed from faith to education." You may think that good education is going to give you high marks in heaven. God does not even look at it.

You may wish that Paul had said, "The righteousness of God is revealed from faith to money." You may think, "I'll buy my way in. I suppose this church could use a little money, so I'll make a contribution." You may give a little money to the church because you are really hoping that God is noticing you. Your money will not help you. God does not want it. If you are trusting anything you have given, then you are trusting in that which will lead to your damnation.

This is why the gospel offends and why people hate the gospel. There is only one thing that pleases God, only one thing that makes God happy. It is not your money. It is not your good works. It is not joining a church.

You can make him happy only by trusting in your heart that His Son died on the cross for all your sins. If you really believe that in your heart, you *have* satisfied his justice; what Luther meant by God's passive justice. God's active justice was satisfied by all Jesus did; his passive justice is satisfied by our faith alone. Therein is the righteousness of God revealed from "faith"—all that Jesus did—"to faith"—our trust in Christ. Trust Him. You say, "Is that it? There must be more!" It is so simple a child can get it. The question is, will you?

All the other religions of the world have this in common, whether Hindu, Muslim, Shintoist, or Buddhist: they are trying to produce a righteousness of their own. The gospel of Jesus Christ is unique in the world religions. Our gospel alone says you must "receive" a righteousness, Jesus's righteousness. It is when you know you cannot bargain with God. When you know that you *cannot* produce the righteousness He requires and that what you *can* produce He *does not* want because our righteousness is "filthy rags" (Isaiah 64:6).

When you admit you have sinned then you can truly see the reason God sent His Son into the world in the first place. It is because you need a Savior. You may know that God sent His Son into the world, but you may have thought it was for somebody else. It is a very humbling thing to have to admit that you need Him; we have all wanted to walk our own way, plough our own furrow, until we realize we are just like everybody else.

The Bible got it right. "All have sinned." What I am asking you to do is to receive a righteousness, Christ's righteousness on your behalf. You do it by acknowledging that you have got no bargaining power, and you say, "God, I have sinned. Wash my sins away by Jesus's blood. I accept the righteousness of Jesus, and trust all that He did plus nothing." Put all of your eggs into one basket. That is making God happy by something you do; just believing Him.

CHAPTER THREE

SAVING FAITH

"The just shall live by faith." (Romans 1:17 KJV)

We now look at the oft-quoted statement, "The just shall live by faith," in order to see its relevance to the doctrine of salvation. It is first found in Habakkuk 2:4 but is quoted three times in the New Testament: Romans 1:17, Galatians 3:11 and Hebrews 10:38 (all KJV).

This statement was vital for the apostle Paul's understanding of justification by faith, the doctrine that was rediscovered by Martin Luther in the sixteenth century. We saw in the last chapter that the first part of Romans 1:17 led Luther to see how faith alone satisfied the passive justice of God. Those who have closely followed Luther's own pilgrimage will know that the last part of this verse was equally important to him: "The just shall live by faith."

Our task however is to discover why this phrase was so important to the apostle Paul. If we ourselves can lay hold of what it was that gripped Paul about Habakkuk's statement, we too will be set afire with a tremendous trust in God. I have been surprised to discover how many Christians have not understood this phrase, not to mention why it was essential to Paul's understanding of salvation.

This verse is so important because it reveals the kind of faith that pleases God, that is, the faith that *saves,* I therefore speak of *saving* faith. I do so in order to distinguish the faith that saves from various types of faith that do not save.

This is one of the most awesome but thrilling verses one can choose to describe saving faith. In Hebrews 11:6 the writer said that without faith it is "impossible" to please God. Think about that! Someone says, "Oh, I'm all right then, I've got faith, I believe in God." One may even say, "I believe in the doctrines of the church." Yet it is possible to give mental assent (head knowledge) and be lost. A lot of people have head knowledge and can say all the right things, "I know I will go to heaven for this or that reason," but not have saving faith.

Some people fancy that they are Christians merely because they believe in God. But the devil believes in God— and trembles (James 2:19 KJV)! There are no atheists in hell. They may have been atheists before they went to hell. But once they are in hell they become total believers in the existence and justice of God. Mere belief in God—as a Supreme Being, First Mover or Higher Power—proves nothing.

Then there is temporal faith. Perhaps you have asked God to help you in a time of need; or when you were in real trouble. You called out to God and felt good and you thought, "Well, I must have faith." General MacArthur used to say, "There are no atheists in foxholes (trenches)." During the Falklands war in 1982 there were many British soldiers who turned to God. Where is their faith today?

The faith that pleases God does not consist of just believing that there is a God. Indeed, if you have no more faith than the devil how could it be that you have faith that saves?

It is very interesting that in the context of the verse in Hebrews that says, "Without faith it is impossible to please him (God)" (Hebrews 11:6 KJV) you have the exact same quotation "The just shall live by faith" (Hebrews 10:38 KJV).

The first line of one of my favorite hymns is "There is life in a look at the Crucified One." C. H. Spurgeon loved to say, "There is life in a look." He based this partly on the words of Jesus, "As Moses lifted up the serpent in the wilderness, even so must the Son of man be lifted up" (John 3:14 KJV). When the Israelites in the wilderness grumbled, God sent venomous snakes that bit the people and they died. People were falling dead everywhere, and panic set in. God told Moses to erect a serpent of brass, then hold it up for the people to see. Those who "looked" at this serpent of brass lived (Numbers 21:9).

Jesus was to be lifted up—on a cross. The phrase "lifted up" was to show how He would die (John 12:32, 33). Not only that; just as the serpent was symbolic of the curse of God placed upon creation as a result of man's sin (Genesis 3:14) so Jesus was made a "curse" for us (Galatians 3:13). Jesus never sinned but was "made" sin for us (2 Corinthians 5:21).

When Jesus compared Himself to the serpent in the wilderness He not only alluded to the saving benefit of His death but also to the nature of saving faith. All one need do is to "look" at the cross! Those who look, live! This is why Spurgeon said, "Come to Jesus. Run to Him, and if you can't run, walk. If you can't walk, crawl. And if you can't crawl, look! For there's life in a look!"

The question we must pose is: how could this be true? It is the reason we have the verse, "The just shall live by faith." It is why the writer of Hebrews quoted Habakkuk 2:4 in the section that ended up saying, "Without faith it is impossible to please him (God)."

The principle of faith that the apostle Paul sets forth is the hardest thing in the world for the natural man to conceive. By "natural man" I mean the way we are without Jesus. You came from your mother's womb, and you have physical life—you can breathe, you can smell, you can taste, you can see, and you can hear. But until a person is converted he is only half a man, only half a person. When Jesus touched a human being He would say, "You are made whole"; and the only way you can be made whole is that new life is infused into you so that you become a new person. It is called conversion. It is called being born again. It is called being saved. To use a theological term, it is called being regenerated.

But even converted people can backslide. Abraham did when he began to worry that faith alone in the promise might not be enough after all. This man had been a sun worshipper. He was natural man, unconverted. God reached him one evening as he was walking out on a clear night, one of those where there are stars visible all over. God said to Abraham, "Count the stars . . . So shall your offspring be." (Genesis 15:5). At the time Abraham did not have a son. He and Sarah were married, but they did not have any children. But God said to Abraham. "You see all the stars. That is how many your seed will engender!"

How many of us, had God said that to us, would have believed it? Most of us—all of us by nature—would say, "Oh, I'd like to believe it. It would be marvelous to believe it. I want to believe it!" But Abraham did believe it, and God looked at Abraham and affirmed him for believing His own word and "counted it to him for righteousness" (Genesis 15:6 KJV).

When the apostle Paul wanted to explain the gospel he likened the way we are saved to exactly the same principle. It was as hard for Abraham to believe that his offspring would be like the stars of the heavens (or as the sand of the seashore) as it is for us to believe that when Jesus died on a cross some 2,000 years ago, in Palestine, just outside Jerusalem, in that moment all of the sins that we have ever committed were put on Him. And yet it is by *believing* this that we are eternally saved.

Do you know what happened to Abraham? He did believe, but a few years later he began to think, "Could it really be true?" Sarah was getting older and older; no child was coming. They wanted to believe God. Sarah had an idea. She said, "Well, there is Hagar my servant girl. You could lie with her, and if she has a son it will be your seed." Abraham did, and Hagar had a son. They named him Ishmael. Abraham was convinced that this was the promised child.

Fourteen years later, when Abraham was nearly a hundred years old, and Sarah in her seventies, Sarah conceived, and Isaac was born. It is a pity that Abraham had that lapse because a lot of trouble came from it—great sorrow. Many Christians started out believing the gospel. They believed their salvation was by the promise alone, but then they thought there has got to be *more* to it. They want to help God out!

At this stage it is necessary to look in some depth at Habakkuk 2:4 to see Paul's priorities. Although most translations of this crucial verse read, "The just shall live by faith," there are no fewer than three valid translations of this verse from the Hebrew. It is one of those verses so pregnant with meaning that no superficial treatment will do.

1. *"The just shall live by his faithfulness"* This is a literal translation. But even this translation contains an intentional ambiguity—apart from the obvious shift from "faith" to

"faithfulness." Because the "his" can be a reference to the believer's own faithfulness but equally to the faithfulness of God, to which we now turn.

2. *"The just shall live by His faithfulness"* The capital "H" is essential here. It is a reference to God's faithfulness. In other words, Habakkuk claimed that the person who lived by the promises of God to keep His word was declared righteous. It is with this very thing in mind that the writer of the epistle to the Hebrews quotes Habakkuk 2:4 in Hebrews 10:38. Having said, "He is faithful that promised" (Hebrews 10:23 KJV), the writer exhorts Hebrew Christians not to lose heart. In Hebrews 10:37 he said, "For yet a little while, And he that shall come will come, and will not tarry" (KJV)—an explicit reference to Habakkuk 2:3: "For the vision is yet for an appointed time, but at the end it shall speak, and not lie: though it tarry, wait for it, because it will surely come, it will not tarry" (KJV).

The writer of Hebrews was saying, "God will intervene—just wait." These Hebrew Christians were urged to hold on, despite God's slowness to step in. This was Habakkuk's original point.

Habakkuk began his prophecy with a complaint. "Why do you tolerate wrong?" (Habakkuk 1:3). It is a common complaint. Why does God permit evil and suffering and gross injustice? Unbelief always poses this question, and so do discouraged Christians. Habakkuk complained not only of God's continual tolerance of evil but of sheer slowness, if not silence, in answering this question.

And yet at the end of Habakkuk's prophecy he said, "I will rejoice in the Lord. . . . The Sovereign Lord is my strength" (Habakkuk 3:18–19). Had things changed? Had God stepped in? On the contrary, Habakkuk said, "Though the fig-tree does not bud . . . and there are no grapes on the vines . . . I will rejoice in the Lord" (Habakkuk 3:17–18). Nothing had changed the things that had led to Habakkuk's original complaint—but something happened to Habakkuk! He saw that God had a secret strategy and that the slowness of its unveiling was planned and purposed. "For the vision is yet for an appointed time . . . though it tarry, wait for it; because it will surely come, it will not tarry" (Habakkuk 2:3 KJV).

There followed this profound statement: "The just (that is, the righteous person) shall live by His (God's) faithfulness." (In the Dead Sea Scrolls of 1947 it was discovered that Habakkuk 2:4 had been understood to read "My righteous one shall live by My faithfulness"—a fairly obvious way it was understood by ancient Hebrews.)

Paul would have known this. It would also follow that he saw this phrase in the context of Habakkuk 2:4, as we ourselves have just seen. It also shows why Paul could say that God's justice is revealed "from faith to faith." For the intentional ambiguity—God's faithfulness and our faith—was the architectural blueprint for Paul's understanding of Christ's faith and our trust. This is what Paul understood Romans 1:17 to mean and why he unraveled it as he did in the successive chapters in Romans.

In a word: the faith that pleases God is a quiet but steadfast confirmation that God will act. Saving faith does not claim to know why God allows evil. But it affirms that God will intervene in the end and, indeed, *has* intervened in Jesus Christ. If we understood the problem of evil we would not need faith at all. But God pronounces that person "just" or "righteous" who lowers his voice, as it were, and simply trusts God's own promise. That is what Habakkuk saw and what became the springboard for Paul's doctrine of salvation.

In Hebrews 10:23 we read, "He is faithful that promised," and you have the warning in Hebrews 10:38, "If any man draw back, my soul shall have no pleasure in him." This describes a man who gives up believing that God will act and thinks, "For a while I believed that it was only trusting the promise, but I now suspect that works have something to do with it." A man once said to me at my church in Fort Lauderdale, "Baptism doesn't save, but it helps." This is a violation of all that Paul is saying. So many simply cannot believe that salvation is by faith alone.

Have you ever asked why God let Hitler thrive? Or Mussolini or Stalin? Why He lets evil men do what they do and step on small men? There are people everywhere that are hurting, and you say, "God if you are there, and you are just and merciful, I don't understand." God says to you, "The vision, the revelation, the disclosure of final justice is for an appointed time; though it tarry, wait for it." There is coming a day when God's pure and ultimate justice will be unveiled.

But most people will not wait, shaking their fists at God, saying, "It's up to us to get justice done in the world."

No Christian should overlook God's requirement to "Act justly and to love mercy" (Micah 6:8). But it is essential to believe above all that God will eventually act. "The vision is for an appointed time . . . but at the end it shall speak . . . though it tarry, wait for it." (Habakkuk 2:3 KJV). It has tarried long. That was written over 600 years before Christ. Almost 2,000 years have passed since. We are talking about almost 2,600 years. And yet a day *is* coming when God's total justice will be unveiled.

The Christian says, "I believe God will act, I don't know when, but I believe it." The non-Christian says, "I don't believe it." The Christian vindicates God now, the non-Christian will vindicate God later—but without faith. Faith is believing without seeing (Hebrews 11:1). The non-Christian will see one day. Such cannot be called faith. The Bible says, "He cometh with clouds; and every eye shall *see* him, and they also which pierced him: and all kindreds of the earth shall wail because of him" (Revelations 1:7 KJV).

Therefore those people in Habakkuk's day (and since) who are persuaded that God will eventually intervene—thus keeping His word—and who consequently live by His faithfulness, are pronounced "just."

The principle working in Habakkuk was true for Abraham. He believed God, and he was justified. Habakkuk said the same thing. Those who believe the promise are vindicating God now. All will see His justice in the end. The Christian sees it now, through the eyes of faith.

Imagine a person who believes that a trustworthy friend is going to call him on the phone. He says "I'm not going to leave the house. I know the phone is going to ring." Someone says, "But you're waiting an awfully long time." "It's all right," he replies. "I believe he's going to ring because he said he would. I trust him." Some believe that Jesus is going to come a second time. But many say, "Where is the promise of His coming? We've heard it for years, he hasn't come yet!" (2 Peter 3:4). But still the faithful say, "He is coming. I believe. I am going to wait!"

Habakkuk's message is that God will act. "The time you wait for this unveiling of justice may be long, but the one who does live by My faithfulness is righteous." So when Paul quoted Habakkuk in Romans 1:17, "The just shall live by faith," he knew he had found a verse that was consistent with what the Holy Spirit had shown him.

3. *"He who is righteous by faith shall live."* This is a third valid translation, emphasizing that "He shall live." It is the promise of eternal life to the one who believes God's word. Thus salvation by faith means life everlasting. It not only points to the quality of life in the here and now, knowing God, as in John 17:3, but to that which lies beyond the grave, as in Luke 18:30.

In a word: heaven below and heaven to come. The Christian is a person who knows God's presence now but also who looks beyond this present life. We know that we are going to heaven when we die. This at bottom is why

Jesus died on the cross. Salvation means heaven—heaven not hell. Our final chapter will bear this out.

This verse also shows three further things about saving faith. First, faith is a persuasion. The one who *sees* that God has spoken indeed is persuaded. The Greek word *pistis* (faith) comes from a root word *peitho* that means "persuade." Faith is when you are so persuaded that nobody can shake you; because you have *seen* it in your heart. You are persuaded that God has spoken; indeed, so much so that you live on and on by the integrity of God.

The second thing is this: the one who is so persuaded is declared righteous. The righteousness of Jesus is transferred to the person who is persuaded of God's promise. God looks over the world and ignores those who are trying to be saved by their works. You can promise to turn over a new leaf; you can give money to the church; you can give all you have to the poor. You can do all those things and God will take no notice. And yet, here is a person who feels so insignificant and unworthy; he hears God's word and something stirs in his heart. He says, "I believe that." And God says, "You are saved. My righteousness I give to you." For the one who is so persuaded is *declared* righteous.

The third thing is that this persuasion is in the *heart*. The apostle Paul went on to say, "The word is nigh thee, even in thy mouth, and *in thy heart*: that is, the word of faith, which we preach; that if thou shalt confess with thy mouth the Lord Jesus, and shalt believe in thine *heart* that God hath raised him from the dead, thou shalt be saved. For with the *heart* man believeth unto righteousness; and with the mouth confession is made unto salvation"

(Romans 10:8–10 KJV). This is not mere mental assent. It is not "head knowledge." You may believe intellectually and be lost. It is not even in the will—by taking refuge in a vow, when in a moment of panic or anxiety you said, "Oh God, I promise from now on."

Some have accepted the idea "God takes the will for the deed." No! It is in the heart where you simply believe the promise. There are people who would be willing that have not believed! They think if they do the things that often prove faith they must have faith. But it is possible for you even to quit your sinning and join the church and your heart never truly be touched. Why? Because this is trying to get God's attention the wrong way. Salvation comes to the one who believes "from the heart"—who is amazed that God would be so gracious as to forgive his sins, and who has entered into a personal knowledge of Jesus's saving work on the cross.

"The just shall live by My faithfulness." The faith that pleases God is quietly believing that God has made a promise and that God will keep it. This is Paul's understanding of the gospel. Habakkuk was concerned with justice and so was Paul. How can a holy, just God forgive guilty, hell-deserving sinners?

This gospel often seems too good to be true. And yet the only ones who can believe it are those in whose hearts the Spirit has worked. Salvation is offered freely to that one who says in the words of the hymn,

> In my hand no price I bring,
> Simply to Thy cross I cling.

CHAPTER FOUR

THE WRATH OF GOD

"For the wrath of God is revealed from heaven against all ungodliness and unrighteousness of men . . ." (Romans 1:18 KJV)

This is possibly the most important chapter of this book. It will point us to the twin truths of why Jesus died on the cross and why we *must* trust His shed blood.

Paul has told his readers he is anxious to come to Rome and reap a harvest there (Romans 1:13). He then expresses a debt to Greeks and non-Greeks and reveals a desire to preach the gospel in Rome (vv. 14–15). At this point he says he is unashamed of the gospel (v. 16) and goes on to outline that gospel in embryonic form (v. 17).

But why this eagerness to preach? Why did Jesus die? And why must people believe? What happens if they do not?

"For . . ." This three-letter word is crucial.

If we omit this word at this juncture we will not only miss the reason God sent His Son to die on the cross in the first place, but also leave out the very reason Paul gave his life spreading the gospel. This man, who said elsewhere "Woe to me if I do not preach the gospel!" (1 Corinthians 9:16 KJV) and "Knowing therefore the terror of the Lord, we persuade men" (2 Corinthians 5:11 KJV), now lets his readers of Rome know the reason for the urgency of this gospel.

It is because of the wrath of God—His *violent anger.* "For the wrath of God is revealed."

Many people are unaware of God's wrath in this matter of salvation. I once asked a well-known publisher of Christian books why they left out the doctrine of hell in one of their important series on Christian doctrines. He replied, "People back off from this as it is so horrifying."

One of the shocks I have had in recent years has been to discover how few ministers preach regularly on eternal punishment any more and the growing number who have subscribed to the teaching of "annihilation." This is a term that denotes extinction of the body and soul rather than the never-ending existence of the same in God's eternity. There was a time when it was largely the cults who subscribed to this; but now it has crept into a sobering number of pulpits—where what is said is good but what is left out is alarming.

Another trend I have observed is the idea that, "If there were no heaven to gain and no hell to shun I'd still be a Christian." Not Paul. He said, "If only for this life we have hope in Christ, we are to be pitied more than all men" (1 Corinthians 15:19 KJV). Not that a Christian is not better off *in this life.* Of course he or she is! But is that the reason Paul gave his life to the spreading of this gospel?

Why was Paul so willing to suffer? "In great endurance; in troubles, hardships and distresses; in beatings, imprisonments and riots; in hard work, sleepless nights and hunger; in purity, understanding, patience and kindness . . . through glory and dishonor, bad report and good report; genuine, yet regarded as imposters; known, yet regarded as unknown; dying, and yet we live on; beaten, and yet not killed" (2 Corinthians 6:4–9).

One fully understands and rejoices that those who evangelize can say, "I have never been so happy; you too can be happy." This is quite right. But that motivation will be short lived if there is not at bottom the very impetus Paul had in explaining and spreading the gospel. For one's evangelism will eventually become superficial and his gospel anemic.

In the nineteenth century missionaries were impelled to leave their comfortable homes and surroundings to go to foreign lands for one simple reason: the heathen were lost and dying without Christ. They went to jungles and to deserts to reach the lost who would otherwise perish forever in hell. They believed this, and it was the main reason they evangelized.

But what often happens is this: because a secondary benefit of conversion is to raise standards of living, the second generation of missionaries often go out and reproduce this effect that conversion causes: they build hospitals, improve agriculture, give medical help—and all those good things. But real conversions tend to become secondary. Why? The vision of hell is blurred.

Thus at the beginning of Paul's epistle to the Romans he states why he is unashamed of the gospel, why Jesus died, why he is ready to preach it in Rome and why it must be *believed:* "For the wrath of God is revealed."

The first time the word "wrath" appears in the New Testament is in Matthew 3:7. The preacher was John the Baptist, of whom Jesus said "Among those that are born of women there is not a greater prophet" (Luke 7:28 KJV). Speaking to Pharisees (self-righteous religious leaders) and Sadducees (those who denied life and punishment beyond the grave) John said, "O generation of vipers, who hath warned you to flee from the wrath to come?" "Whoever believes in the Son," he preached, "has eternal life, but whoever rejects the Son will not see life, for God's wrath remains on him" (John 3:36 KJV).

Essential to the message of the first preacher of the New Testament, then, was "Flee from the wrath to come." John warned that we should run from God's wrath as soon as possible because some day everybody who did not do this in sufficient time will try to do it—without success. The last writer in the New Testament—John the beloved disciple—described people who saw the revelation of God's wrath too late. "Then the kings of the earth, the princes, the generals, the rich, the mighty, and every slave and every free man hid in caves and among the rocks of the mountains. They called to the mountains and the rocks, 'Fall on us and hide us from the face of him who sits on the throne and from the wrath of the Lamb! For the great day of their wrath has come, and who can stand?'" (Revelations 6:15–17).

One day every one of us will see Jesus. To some it will be the loveliest sight that ever was in the world. "We shall be like him; for we shall see him as he is" (1 John 3:2). This, however, describes only those who are saved. And yet everybody will, nonetheless, see Jesus. "Look, he is coming with the clouds, and every eye will see him, even those who pierced him; and all the peoples of the earth will mourn because of him. So shall it be! Amen" (Revelations 1:7). Therefore if you are not saved that is one face you most certainly are not going to want to see.

It is strange how Jesus is admired by so many. They claim He was a good man and a good teacher. But Jesus had more to say about the wrath of God than any writer in the New Testament! What is more, Jesus went into detail to *describe the pains* one will experience from God's coming wrath. Hell has been called a place of "darkness, where there will be weeping and gnashing of teeth" (Matthew 8:12); "the fiery furnace, where there will be weeping and gnashing of teeth" (Matthew 13:42). "It is better for you to enter life maimed or crippled than to have two hands or two feet and be thrown into eternal fire" (Matthew 18:8). "Depart from me, you who are cursed, into the eternal fire prepared for the devil and his angels" (Matthew 25:41).

Martin Luther called John 3:16 "The Bible in a nutshell." John 3:16 demonstrates why Jesus died and what will *not* happen to those who believe: "For God so loved the world that he gave his one and only Son, that whoever believes in him *shall not perish* but have eternal life."

Eternal punishment for those who do not believe in the Son was an assumption underlying all Jesus taught. His coming into the world did not create hell. Those who take the gospel to the heathen do not create hell for them. All men are condemned anyway. "Whoever does not believe stands condemned already" (John 3:18). I do not understand it. But this is His teaching.

It is not for you or me to criticize this teaching. We may not like it. I, for one, do not like it. I did not originate it, I would never have thought of it. Let us lower our voices and adopt the spirit and word of Abraham when he saw Sodom's impending doom: "Will not the Judge of all the earth do right?" (Genesis 18:25).

Ludwig Feuerbach, the nineteenth-century German philosopher whose teaching anticipated Marxism, said that God was nothing more than man's projection upon the backdrop of the universe. His idea was that man needs to believe there is "one out there who cares and who will reward us with Heaven when we die."

I ask, who among men would have ever thought up the idea of hell? Ask any man if he likes the idea of hell.

Many feel contemptuous of it, many hate it and the God who thought it up. Hell is God's idea. He is the one who created it, originally, if I understand Matthew 25:41, for the devil and his angels.

Paul got his doctrine from Jesus (Galatians 1:12). When Paul addressed Felix, his message was a discourse on "righteousness, self-control and the judgment to come." Felix trembled (Acts 24:25). But I fear that few people tremble at preaching today. According to Paul this is why Jesus died; we are justified "by his blood" to be "saved from God's wrath through him" (Romans 5:9). It is Jesus who will some day be "revealed from heaven in blazing fire" and "will punish those who . . . do not obey the gospel of our Lord Jesus. They will be punished with everlasting destruction and shut out from the presence of the Lord" (2 Thessalonians 1:7–9).

Notice that Paul says, "For the wrath of God *is* revealed." He might have said "will be revealed," for it will be unveiled to all on the Last Day. But in what sense is it revealed already?

It is revealed in the gospel itself. For Paul knows of no other gospel but that which inherently contains God's wrath. If the gospel is the declaration of God's love only, it will not effectually communicate the reason Jesus died or why He is to be believed.

One Sunday evening Dr. James Dobson, known for "Focus on the Family," came into my vestry after a gospel service. I did not know what the reaction of this famous man would be to a gospel sermon which had just emphasized both the justice and mercy of God. So many psychologists today speak only of love and acceptance and say little about correction and toughness. But he gave me a fresh illustration. "Take the battery of a car. If you connect the cable to the negative only you can put a hand on it and feel nothing. Or connect the other cable to the positive alone and again you will feel nothing. But if you connect to *both*, the electricity flows and the effect is dynamic. What is needed in the pulpit today is a message that emphasizes both the love and wrath of God. One without the other is impotent."

The wrath of God is revealed in Paul's gospel. Why? Because of what Jesus suffered on the cross. The wrath of God was poured out upon Jesus. At some point between twelve o'clock noon and three o'clock on Good Friday Jesus cried out, "My God, my God, why have you forsaken me?" (Matthew 27:46). This is when our sins were transferred from us to Him (Isaiah 53:6; 2 Corinthians 5:21). If you want to know how much God hates sin, look at the cross. If there were no such thing as God's wrath Jesus would never have died on the cross. "The wages of sin is death" (Romans 6:23). Jesus never sinned so He ought not to have died. Why *did* He die? Our sins were put on Him, and God punished Him so we might be saved from His wrath (Romans 5:9).

After all, if all that God wants from us is a mere change of life there would be no need to punish His Son. God could achieve morality and clean living in other ways. The Law of Moses produced morality—through fear of punishment. But that is not what the gospel is all about. The only way

God can be satisfied is by total sinlessness—which Jesus produced—and by a righteous substitute—which Jesus was. Jesus alone is Savior. I could never produce the righteousness God requires. The standard is too high: sinlessness in thought, word, and deed sixty seconds a minute, sixty minutes an hour, twenty-four hours a day, three hundred and sixty-five days a year! Jesus met the standard. "It is because of him that you are in Christ Jesus, who has become for us wisdom from God—that is, our righteousness, holiness and redemption" (1 Corinthians 1:30).

There is yet another reason why Paul said, "For the wrath of God is revealed": to make us conscious of sin. For the gospel *will* produce a change of life. This comes when we see something of God's attitude towards sin. For when one receives Jesus as Savior he receives Him also as Lord. You acknowledge Jesus as Lord in two ways. First, you see Him as the God-man. Jesus was God in the flesh (John 1:1, 14). He was God as though He were not man, and man as though He were not God. When we confess Jesus as Lord we acknowledge Him as God. That is the meaning of Romans 10:9: "That if you confess with your mouth, 'Jesus is Lord,' and believe in your heart that God raised him from the dead, you will be saved."

But we also acknowledge Him as Master. "Under new management" is a good way of putting it. This does not mean perfection or perfect submission to all that God finally wants of us when we become Christians. But because there will be such a consciousness of sin when we sense how God feels toward sin, a change of life will follow. It comes more quickly for some than for others. But holiness is the inevitable result of genuine conversion. "Make every effort to live in peace with all men and to be holy; without holiness no one will see the Lord" (Hebrews 12:14).

If the wrath of God is not preached in the context of "good news" the motivation to holiness will likely be lacking. When I see that it is my sin that nailed Jesus to the cross it will affect my life. No repentance, no salvation.

Never think that the wrath of God is not a good motive either to become a Christian or produce holiness. Some may feel it is "beneath them" to be motivated by God's anger. But are we wiser than God? Are we so self-righteous? We *do* need to see and feel what God feels before we will truly be what He wants us to be.

It was the love of God that moved Him to send His Son. "For God so loved the world that he gave his one and only Son" (John 3:16). It is equally the love of God that moved Him to *tell* us of the coming wrath. One does you no favor not to tell you this.

Those who believe in annihilation usually build their case on the so-called doctrine of conditional immortality. Their view is that one is not given immortality by creation but only by regeneration (conversion). They say that God alone is immortal (and that of course is true) but that this immortality is the gift of being born again, not what man is naturally endowed with by creation. I reply: God made us after His own image (Genesis 1:26, 27) and immortality is given by creation.

Such people also like to believe that the Greek word that is translated "perish" in John 3:16 means extinction.

That means you become nothing—as though you had never been born. But the Greek word there does not mean that, it means "useless." A car may be "written off," as they say, but it is all there. If extinction is the ultimate consequence of not believing the gospel, why would Jesus say of Judas Iscariot, "It would be better for him if he had not been born" (Matthew 26:24), one of Jesus's strongest affirmations of never-ending punishment in the age to come.

But Judas was born. And God has implanted upon every person His own image. God is immortal and can never die. He chose to make man different from dogs and cats. When animals die, that is the end. When man dies, it is the beginning of a new and never-ending existence in eternity.

There are three stages of the revelation of God's wrath. The first is by His *word*. That has been implied throughout this chapter. His word plainly tells you and me that God is angry with sin. "The wrath of God is revealed from heaven against all ungodliness and unrighteousness."

The second stage is *when God does nothing* about one's sin. He just lets people continue in sin—and feel nothing. The severest kind of punishment for sin in this life is God's silent judgment. Sometimes God steps down from heaven and brings a gracious judgment. This is when he is not silent about how He feels. But should God choose to remain silent when He looks at one's sin it is a very ominous sign indeed. His silence is a hint that God will simply wait until the Final Day.

The remainder of Romans 1 is a sobering description of God's anger with sin. Three times Paul says "God gave them up" (Romans 1:24, 26, 28). He does not say God "pushed" them or "hammered" them. He just gave them over to do awful things. God punished them in the here and now by letting them have their own way. But that is not the end of the matter.

God has time on His side, and He can wait. If one is able to sin and feel nothing—no guilt, no chastening, no sense of God's displeasure—it could mean that God is very angry indeed. God never loses His temper. He is "slow to anger" (Psalm 103:8). But when He is very angry indeed He has the capacity to wait, unlike most of us.

He waits for the final stage of the revealing of His wrath: the *judgment to come.* It is man's destiny to die; after that, "the judgment" (Hebrews 9:27). "Then I saw a great white throne and him who was seated on it. Earth and sky fled from his presence, and there was no place for them. And I saw the dead, great and small, standing before the throne, and books were opened. Another book was opened, which is the book of life. The dead were judged according to what they had done as recorded in the books. The sea gave up the dead that were in it, and death and Hades gave up the dead that were in them, and each person was judged according to what he had done. Then death and Hades were thrown into the lake of fire. The lake of fire is the second death. If anyone's name was not found written in the book of life, he was thrown into the lake of fire" (Revelations 20:11–15).

52

It will be an awful day. It is the Omega Point towards which all history is moving. It has been described many ways in the Bible. The Old Testament prophets saw it coming. It has been called the "day of the Lord" (Joel 3:14; Amos 5:18). It is called "that day" (Matthew 7:22), "the last day" (John 12:48), "the day" (Romans 2:16), "a day" (Acts 17:31), "the day of our Lord Jesus Christ" (1 Corinthians 1:8), "the day of Jesus Christ" (Philippians 1:6), "the day of judgment" (2 Peter 2:9), and "the day of God" (2 Peter 3:12).

May I share this principle: the longer God waits in executing His wrath, the greater the punishment will be. "Because the Lord disciplines those whom he loves, and he punishes everyone he accepts as a son" (Hebrews 12:6). Sometimes it is true that the more deeply God feels, the longer He waits. In our impatience we find waiting almost unbearable. God is the opposite of man. He waits. God will have His day.

It is my prayer that the reader will never experience the wrath of God described in this book—save for its being revealed "on paper" by His word, and in your heart by the Holy Spirit. It is my hope that the Holy Spirit will use this little book and grip you and bring you to your knees; that you will cry out to Him. What is it you must ask for? Mercy. This is what people in hell will ask for—too late. A man in hell (described by Jesus himself) cried, "Have mercy on me, and send Lazarus, that he may dip the tip of his finger in water, and cool my tongue; for I am tormented in this flame" (Luke 16:24).

Ask for mercy now. I close with a plea that you utter this prayer from your heart:

Lord Jesus, have mercy upon me. I need you. I want you. I am sorry for my sins. Wash my sins away by your blood. I welcome your Holy Spirit into my heart. I receive you as my Savior and my Lord. I thank you for saving me. Amen.